The
FEAST

The

FEAST

Reflections on the Bread of Life

Gregory Post
& Charles Turner

[signature: Charles Turner]

HarperSanFrancisco
A Division of HarperCollins Publishers

Acknowledgments begin on page 145.

FIRST EDITION

Library of Congress Cataloging-in-Publication Data
Post, Gregory.
   The feast : meditations on the bread of life / Gregory Post &
Charles Turner. — 1st ed.
      p.   cm.
   ISBN 0–06–066689–7
   1. Bread—Religious aspects—Christianity—Meditations.
2. Lord's Supper—Bread—Meditations.   3. Lord's Supper—
Meditations.
I. Turner, Charles.   II. Title.
BV825.52.P67   1992
242—dc20   91–59030
                                                                         CIP

92 93 94 95 96 97 ❖ HAD 10 9 8 7 6 5 4 3 2 1

This edition is printed on acid-free paper that meets the American
National Standards Institute Z39.48 Standard.

For
Virginia Thomas Schaefer
1913–1990

The danger is not lest the soul should doubt whether there is any bread, but lest, by a lie, it should persuade itself that it is not hungry.

Simone Weil,
Waiting for God

Contents

Preface

Greg Post and I share certain preoccupations that transcend the gap in our ages. Our friendship thrives on two in particular. We both like to eat. We both like to contemplate the visible world as a reflection of the invisible world. One day we got to talking about how the goodness of food and the goodness of God are parts of the same cloth, and we got carried away and started planning this book.

We do not present a linear, systematized discourse. We do not encourage the reader toward a truth to chew up and spit out, but one to be tasted and savored. We have chosen a thematic approach, even a discursive and leisurely one, with allusions to (and excerpts from) Holy Writ and other writ as well. I with my bookish leanings hold forth in part 1; Greg with his theological insights, in part 2. Part 3 is a collaboration.

We trust that this book will be an interesting read in itself, but our main prayer is that it will serve as an appetizer, inviting all to "taste and see that the Lord is good."

Charles Turner

The
FEAST

Part One
FOOD FOR THE JOURNEY

$\mathcal{B}$read is the mystery of our existence. That is why Christ teaches us to pray for our daily ration. One cannot imagine a more practical request. Without nourishment in the mystery of our existence, we die.

My reference is visible bread, smellable bread, chewable bread, bread that will become waste. All true mystery is a down-to-earth business. Only as we begin to appreciate our given metaphors for what they are in themselves do we begin to appreciate their corresponding realities. Sometimes we emphasize a theology of spiritual bread to the extent that we de-emphasize a theology of physical bread. We counter the nature of the Incarnation when we do. The worst of the blunder is that we exalt a lopsided Christ. Sad to say, we who believe in the Incarnation can be as tempted by abstractions as anyone else. Unless we return again and again in faith to the tangible edges of everyday mystery, we disrespect the substance of things not seen.

A doctrine of bodily nourishment is rampant in Holy Scripture. The fact that the Lord feeds his people is demonstrated throughout both Testaments. The theme is easy to overlook because it seems so mundane. Having designed our bodies to require fuel, the Creator provides that necessity. His benevolence here is consistent with the pattern of grace in which the demands of his law are met by the provisions of his gospel.

The wonder of food is beautifully expressed in the Hebrew meal berakoth: "Blessed art thou, Yahweh, our God, King of the Universe, who bringest forth bread from the earth." This table prayer was used in the years that Christ walked upon our planet. It is probably the blessing that he himself offered on a regular basis.

With redeemed imaginations, we can almost hear him speak the words—in our own language, no less, for such is the kingdom in which we listen. Because bread is bread from one generation to another, we can almost get a whiff of the very loaves he blessed.

Nothing says "home" more appealingly than the earthy frankincense of bread fresh from the oven. A peasant comes home from the field and the promise reaches out through the open door. A stockbroker returns in the evening to his high-rise condo and finds it transformed by the same miracle of basic domesticity. The second example is less likely than the first but, thanks be to God, still possible. Mennonites tell us that the surest way to sell a house is to have bread baking in the kitchen when prospective buyers arrive. The aroma of bread triggers a mood of shelter and sanctuary. Perhaps that is why it welcomes so warmly those who are away from home, be they dinner guests from across town or wayfarers from a distant land.

Recorded in Genesis is a foundational instance of hospitality involving food and drink. Abram had come out of battle victorious and was journeying homeward. Melchizedek, King of Salem, went out to meet him and brought bread and wine. He blessed Abram and said:

"Blessed be Abram
by God Most High,
creator of heaven and earth.
And blessed be God Most High
who has delivered your enemies into your power."

Genesis 14:19–20, NEB

Melchizedek, though identified as a priest of God Most High, is a rather mysterious personage. The details of his life are minimal but impressive. Our ignorance of him somehow adds to his aura, especially when we read in the New Testament letter to the Hebrews: "He has no father, no mother, no lineage; his years have no beginning, his life no end. He is like the Son of God. He remains a priest for all time" (7:3, NEB). Whatever we perceive from this puzzling biographical sketch, Melchizedek was at least a symbol of preeminent dignity. His coming forth with bread and wine, prophetic in itself when we think of the Eucharist, was no doubt characterized by more pomp than the picnics we know, but it was first of all an act of practical hospitality in which a warrior and his men were welcomed and refreshed.

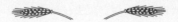

*B*read is hope, bread is encouragement, bread is strength. Bread never speaks of the grave, is not sentimental about despair. Even a stale ration of this mystery can, crust by crust, wage a valiant campaign against starvation.

More than once during life in the camps, Shukov had recalled the way they used to eat in his village: whole pots full of potatoes, pans of oatmeal, and, in the early days, big chunks of meat. And milk enough to bust their guts. That wasn't the way to eat, he learned in camp. You had to eat with all your mind on the food—like now, nibbling the bread bit by bit, working the crumbs up into a paste with your tongue and sucking it into your cheeks. And how good it tasted—that soggy black bread!

One Day in the Life of Ivan Denisovich
Alexandr Solzhenitsyn

I don't think I ever met anybody who didn't like the taste of bread. I have known persons to give it up in order to lose weight (a questionable method unless a physician prescribes), but those individuals, in common with celibates, knew they were abstaining from something delectable. We can make a fair assumption that our peasant coming in from the field, though he be lusting for his wife, will follow his nose to the table before he follows his lust to the bed. That presumably would be the sequence with our stockbroker as well, no matter how topsy-turvy are modern lives. The choreography of these gratifications has more to do with primal instinct than cultural habit. Although it is possible to remain celibate throughout one's life, one cannot go without nourishment for very long if one wishes to stay alive. The Greek philosopher Democritus is said to have proposed that the very smelling of hot bread could add to a person's longevity.

Literature down through the ages has celebrated bread as the lifegiver that it is. This recurring metaphor—bread as life itself—is so powerful that our contemporary literature, much of which has embraced despair as its theme, continues to honor it. That Holy Scripture and other literature should coincide on this matter ought not to surprise us, for truth is truth, without bounds, and truth perpetuates its own aesthetics.

In one of Raymond Carver's short stories, conflict erupts between a baker and a couple whose child has died as the result of an accident. The mother has not picked up the birthday cake she ordered for the child, and the baker, unaware of the intervening tragedy, makes harassing telephone calls. Tension increases because he does not identify himself. When the mother finally realizes who the caller is, she and her husband drive to the shopping center for a midnight confrontation. The baker does more than back down, does more than express sympathy. He begs forgiveness. He becomes flesh and blood.

"You probably need to eat something," the baker said. "I hope you'll eat some of my rolls. You have to eat and keep going. Eating is a small good thing in a time like this," he said.

He served them cinnamon rolls just out of the oven, the icing still runny. He put butter on the table and knives to spread the butter. Then the baker sat down at the table with them. He waited. He waited until they each took a roll from the platter and began to eat. "It's good to eat something," he said, watching them. "There's more. Eat up. Eat all you want. There's all the rolls in the world in here."

They ate rolls and drank coffee. Ann was suddenly hungry, and the rolls were warm and sweet. She ate three of them, which pleased the baker. Then he began to talk. They listened carefully. Although they were tired and in anguish, they listened to what the baker had to say. They nodded when the baker began to speak of loneliness, and of the sense of doubt and limitation that had come to him in his middle years. He told them what it was like to be childless all these years. To repeat the days with the ovens endlessly full and endlessly empty. The party food, the celebrations he'd worked over. Icing knuckle-deep. The wedding couples stuck into cakes. Hundreds of them, no, thousands of them. Birthdays. Just imagine all those candles burning. He had a necessary trade. He was a baker. He was glad he wasn't a florist. It was better to be feeding people. This was a better smell anytime than flowers.

"Smell this," the baker said, breaking open a dark loaf. "It's a heavy bread, but rich." They smelled it, then he had them taste it. It had the taste of molasses and coarse grains. They listened to him. They ate what they could. They swallowed the dark bread. It was like daylight under the fluorescent trays of light. They talked on into the early morning, the high, pale cast of light in the window, and they did not think of leaving.

A Small, Good Thing
Raymond Carver

Within hours after a death, in many neighborhoods, friends are likely to drop by with gifts of food. This practice might be losing ground in our society, but I can remember that the women of my childhood got down to serious cake baking when death paid a visit nearby. I remember wondering, "Why gifts of food when people are sad?" Food—cakes especially—seemed festive and out of place in an atmosphere of grief. Not until I was thirty-five, when my mother died and a procession of turkey and ham and casseroles invaded the house, did the custom make sense. Out-of-town guests were to be fed. My family was relieved of heavy cooking, and in the practicality of it all, there was no delicatessen expense. Furthermore—and this came as rather a surprise—I found that I was hungry. I remember another death in the family when my daughter and I came in from the funeral and, after declaring we weren't hungry, went straight to the kitchen and devoured newly arrived peas, one entire offering, straight from the bowl.

That occasion came back to me when I read those last paragraphs of Carver's short story. Except for the fact of a death, the circumstances were dissimilar, and yet hunger was there. Sometimes when we think that food is the last thing we are interested in, we are in fact deeply hungry. Healthy grief is ravenous for life. Healthy grief knows instinctively that food is necessary.

"No one ever told me that grief felt so much like fear," wrote C. S. Lewis, describing in *A Grief Observed* the dark tunnel through which he passed after the death of his wife. The sentence startles with its rightness. The sensation of grief *is* like fear, we know, those of us who have lost loved ones.

Grief, fear, depression. These emotions are closely related and are common to all of our journeys. Holy Scripture, in contrast to its mighty array of wonders and miracles, zooms in revealingly on difficult human situations. Its majestic phrasing never glosses over the low points in the lives of its heroes. The prophet Elijah became so fearful under Jezebel's threat that he sat down and wished for death. That is depression at its most articulate level.

When he reached Beersheba in Judah, he left his servant there and himself went a day's journey into the wilderness. He came upon a broom-bush, and sat down under it and prayed for death. . . . He lay down under the bush and, while he slept, an angel touched him and said, "Rise and eat." He looked, and there at his head was a cake baked on hot stones, and a pitcher of water. He ate and drank and lay down again. The angel of the Lord came again and touched him a second time, saying, "Rise and eat; the

journey is too much for you." He rose and ate
and drank and, sustained by this food, he went
on for forty days and forty nights to Horeb, the
mount of God.

1 Kings 19:3–8, NEB

Had the destination bannered less symbolism,
that's still not bad mileage for a cake baked on hot
stones.

*W*e are dealing with generic terminology, of course. Let us hope that "our daily bread" includes meat and potatoes and other components of a well-balanced diet. But in line with biblical precedent, these reflections employ the staple foodstuff to represent the whole gamut of things to eat and drink. For some reason in the mind of God, bread addresses human hunger with greater pertinence than any other food. Had Jean Valjean in Victor Hugo's *Les Miserables* stolen a bowl of stew to save his sister's child from starvation, the drama would have been lessened. That the theft was of bread added compass to the novel as surely as did the volume of pages.

One of the last entries in *The Journals of John Cheever* ties right in with our theme. "Feeling that I have conquered cancer, I stroll around the house. A loaf of bread is needed, and I will search for one. What more simple and universal pursuit could there be than a man looking for a new loaf of bread? . . . For me the bakery is the heart—and sometimes the soul—of a village!" Nowhere did Cheever the accomplished fiction writer express his insights more deeply (or his quandaries more poignantly) than in the account of his personal life. Because this focus on bread appears when death is closing in, it achieves the solemnity of a testament.

When we speak of bread as bread, we speak of many things. It is a form of nourishment that calls up a litany of variations within its own category: baguettes, tortillas, Parkerhouse rolls, hamburger buns, soda crackers, muffins, white bread, whole wheat bread, limpa, lahvosh, challah, pita, pumpernickel, corn pone. The list encircles the earth. We can be certain there are many breads we would not recognize as members of that family. "What is that?" we might ask if we came upon one of unfamiliar appearance and texture. The question resounds the perplexity of the Israelites when they first came upon manna, the miraculous food by which God fed them during their years in the wilderness.

> When the dew was gone, there in the wilderness, fine flakes appeared, fine as hoar-frost on the ground. When the Israelites saw it, they said to one another, "What is that?," because they did not know what it was. Moses said to them, "That is the bread which the LORD has given you to eat."
>
> Exodus 16:14–15, NEB

Biblical studies indicate that the word *manna* is but a statement of the question, "What is that?" Surely the most unusual bread in one sense, it was in another sense the mere standard. Not only did it answer the whines of a hungering people at a given time, at a point where history and myth continue to intersect, it provided an illustration for the ages. Manna was the keynote when Christ taught the lesson of bread. He used it as one of many stepping-stones to lead us from smug ignorance to a knowledge of the way things really are.

Manna was described as tasting like wafers made with honey, but the romance of it all was tempered by a certain amount of labor. The flakes had to be gathered and measured and used according to instructions. There was baking and boiling and storing for the sabbath. With the miracle came responsibilities. Human involvement was required.

Bread and the sweat of the brow have always been affiliated, and the concept of *tender* is an outcome of the association. That is why *bread* and *money* are sometimes interchangeable terms in the idiom of the streets. The relationship is taut enough to prevent confusion, yet even the sidewalk philosopher knows that in the long run bread is more valuable than money. The man who falls into an abandoned mine shaft and will not be rescued for days would do better to have with him a loaf of bread than a checkbook. In dire situations, nourishment is the wealth that finance is not.

A misadventure more common today is dramatized by Jay McInerney in *Bright Lights, Big City.* The protagonist of this hip parable is a young man in Manhattan who, though he's had everything going for him, is suffering "a creeping sense of mortality" as he nears the bottom of his plunge into chemical euphoria. Awed by a friend's "strict refusal to acknowledge any goal higher than the pursuit of pleasure," he has fallen for a way of life that robs him of all that is good and true and solid. The structure of the novel is a week-long dialogue with his own consciousness. At the end, which is almost the end of himself, he stumbles out of a party, out of a scene, into the morning of the first day of the week.

You're not sure exactly where you are going. You don't feel you have the strength to walk home. You walk faster. If the sunlight catches you on the streets, you will undergo some terrible chemical change.

After a few minutes you notice the blood on your fingers. You hold your hand up to your face. There is blood on your shirt, too. You find a Kleenex in your pocket and hold it to your nose. You advance with your head tilted back against your shoulders.

By the time you reach Canal Street, you think that you will never make it home. You look for taxis. A bum is sleeping under the awning of a shuttered shop. As you pass he raises his head and says, "God bless you and forgive your sins." You wait for the cadge but it doesn't come. You wish he hadn't said anything.

As you turn, what is left of your olfactory equipment sends a message to your brain: fresh bread. Somewhere they are baking bread. You

can smell it, even through the nose bleed. You
see bakery trucks loading in front of a building
on the next block. You watch as bags of rolls are
carried out onto the loading dock by a man with
tattooed forearms. This man is already at work
so that normal people can have fresh bread for
their morning tables. The righteous people who
sleep at night and eat eggs for breakfast. It is
Sunday morning and you haven't eaten since
. . . when? Friday night. As you approach, the
smell of bread washes over you like a gentle
rain. You inhale deeply, filling your lungs. Tears
come to your eyes, and you feel such a rush of
tenderness and pity that you stop by a lamppost
and hang for support.

The smell of bread recalls you to another
morning. You arrived home from college after
driving half the night; you just felt like coming
home. When you walked in, the kitchen was
steeped in the same aroma. Your mother asked
what the occasion was, and you said a whim.

You asked if she was baking. "Learning to draw inferences at college, are we," you remember her asking. She said she had to find some way to keep herself busy now that her sons were taking off. You said that you hadn't left, not really. You sat down at the kitchen table to talk, and the bread soon started to burn. She had made bread only two other times that you could recall. Both times it had burned. You remember being proud of your mother then for never having submitted to the tyranny of the kitchen, for having other things on her mind. She cut you two thick slices of bread anyway. They were charred on the outside but warm and moist inside.

You approach the tattooed man on the loading dock. He stops working and watches you. There is something wrong with the way your legs are moving. You wonder if your nose is still bleeding.

"Bread." This is what you say to him, although you meant to say something more.

"What was your first clue?" he says. He is a man who has served his country, you think, a man with a family somewhere outside the city.

"Could I have some? A roll or something?"

"Get outa here."

"I'll trade you my sunglasses," you say. You take off your shades and hand them to him. "Ray-Bans. I lost the case." He tries them on, shakes his head a few times and then takes them off. He folds the glasses and puts them in his shirt pocket.

"You're crazy," he says. Then he looks back into the warehouse. He picks up a bag of hard rolls and throws it at your feet.

You get down on your knees and tear open the bag. The smell of warm dough envelops you. The first bite sticks in your throat and you almost gag. You will have to go slowly. You will have to learn everything over again.

Bright Lights, Big City
Jay McInerney

This is not the case of an author snatching for a symbol to tack on. Subtle whiffs of yeast emanate from passages throughout the book, so that this final desperate devouring falls into place and belongs. Were the allusions to baked goods woven into the narrative to achieve this perfectly valid effect? Or was the motif discovered during the writing, in the ordinary touches that were natural in the periphery—the seeming periphery—of the story? Perhaps McInerney himself does not know for sure. I would hold with the latter, for I suspect that the larger part of any creative process is discovery and not imposition.

But is this too much weight to put on bread as a symbol? No. It works. Even the part about getting down on his knees. It works because the significance of bread is really there. Existentially. The strength of this metaphor is not so astonishing when we consider that Moses instructed Aaron to place a container of manna in the presence of the Lord to be kept for future generations. Following up, the author of the letter to the

Hebrews lists a golden jar of manna among the contents of the ark of the covenant. That is worth thinking about: Bread had a place in the Holy of Holies.

Has a place in the Holy of Holies, for those of us who believe. Which sort of changes the character of the bread we break each day. The hint is that we partake of far more than the listed ingredients. And then there's the further hint, that even to touch bread is somehow a priestly act.

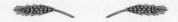

$\mathcal{P}$salm 136, the Great Hallel, was designed to be sung antiphonally in the temple. A liturgical psalm if there ever was one, it is repetitive and monotonous unless we discipline our minds to the text and involve our imaginations in the history it recounts. If we catch it like a wave and ride it, we find that the pulsing interruptions of praise actually sustain the theme as it gathers and swells toward what is surely one of the loftiest peaks in Holy Scripture.

It is good to give thanks to the Lord,
for his love endures for ever.

Give thanks to the God of gods;
    his love endures for ever.
Give thanks to the Lord of lords;
    his love endures for ever.
Alone he works great marvels;
    his love endures for ever.
In wisdom he made the heavens;
    his love endures for ever.
He laid the earth upon the waters;
    his love endures for ever.
He made the great lights,
    his love endures for ever,
the sun to rule by day,
    his love endures for ever,
the moon and the stars to rule by night;
    his love endures for ever.
He struck down the first-born of the Egyptians,
    his love endures for ever,
and brought Israel from among them;
    his love endures for ever.

With strong hand and outstretched arm,
   his love endures for ever,
he divided the Red Sea in two,
   his love endures for ever,
and made Israel to pass through it,
   his love endures for ever;
but Pharaoh and his host he swept into the sea;
   his love endures for ever.
He led his people through the wilderness;
   his love endures for ever.
He slew mighty kings,
   his love endures for ever,
Sihon king of the Amorites,
   his love endures for ever,
and Og the king of Bashan;
   his love endures for ever.
He gave their land to Israel,
   his love endures for ever,
to Israel his servant as their patrimony;
   his love endures for ever.

He remembered us when we were cast down,
    his love endures for ever,
and rescued us from our enemies;
    his love endures for ever.
He gives food to all his creatures;
    his love endures for ever.
Give thanks to the God of heaven,
    for his love endures for ever.

Psalm 136, NEB

One danger in the reading of this psalm is to commemorate the mighty acts of God that constitute the buildup and then to dismiss the pinnacle as anti-climactic. *He gives food to all his creatures:* If that is ho-hum, we ought to fast a good long fast and come back prepared and read the psalm again. Import does not wane in the final four lines, and the concluding call for thanksgiving is not there for purely structural purposes. The writer knew what he was doing. Just as an entertainer saves the best act for last, and just as the novelist does not reveal where all is leading until the end, a poet chooses very carefully the words that will (as T. S. Eliot phrased in "Burnt Norton") "reach into the silence."

God's feeding of his creatures is not a lesser act than creation or redemption. It is an enterprise of the same energy from which those movements flow. Creation is an onward event—there is the child that is being conceived at this moment, the rose that is opening, the melody that is wooing the composer. And redemption, though radiating through the specific event of the cross, is not tethered to the day of the nails and the wood—it was present in the great Passover and is expressed repeatedly into our midst today by Word and Sacrament. Creation continues and redemption continues, but the act of feeding continues with a more insistent rhythm—three meals a day for many of us—and on a plane we can more easily comprehend.

The goodness of God is not abstract when we sit down to eat. It doesn't have to be Trout Margery at Galatoire's in New Orleans. It can be a hamburger and fries at the local McDonald's. Grace is depicted before us, and of grace we partake. It is visible and tangible. It is tasty.

The Creator routinely meets us on a sensual level. Food is provided for our pleasure as well as for our nourishment. Pleasure, along with every gift that comes down from the Father of Lights, is holy—until indulged in outside his holy law, and then it becomes an end in itself and not an avenue for his glory. There are warnings against gluttony, of course, just as there are warnings against that kindred selfishness called adultery. But we trip into the ancient heresy of Gnosticism when we think of physical pleasure as having no spiritual substance. It is precisely because of imbedded spirituality that rules and signals are necessary. The Christian who thinks of all physical pleasure as "worldly" blunders as profoundly as the hedonist. One misses the boat in one direction, the other in the other. When our focus is true, we can sing Lionel Bart's "Food, Glorious Food" with the same gusto that the orphans sang it in the musical *Oliver!* We can accent the word *glorious* and know we've got it right in more ways than one.

On a less rousing note, we can reflect appreciatively on the experience of a French aviator who, en route from Paris to Saigon in the days before World War II, crashed into the Sahara desert. Although best known as the author of *The Little Prince,* he wrote himself into my "scrapbook of connections" with his account of the time that he and his mechanic, Prevort, kept their own appointment in the wilderness.

A man can go nineteen hours without water, and what have we drunk since last night? A few drops of dew at dawn. But the northeast wind is still blowing, still slowing up the process of our evaporation. To it, also, we owe the continuous accumulation of high clouds. If only they would drift straight overhead and break into rain! But it never rains in the desert.

"Look here, Prevort. Let's rip up one of the parachutes and spread the sections on the ground, weighed down with stones. If the wind stays in the same quarter till morning, they'll catch the dew and we can wring them out into one of the tanks."

We spread six triangular sections of parachute under the stars, and Prevort unhooked a fuel tank. This was as much as we could do for ourselves until dawn. But, miracle of miracles! Prevort had come upon an orange while working over the tank. We shared it, and though it was little enough to men who could have used a few gallons of sweet water, still I was overcome with relief.

Stretched out beside the fire I looked at the glowing fruit and said to myself that men did not know what an orange was. "Here we are, condemned to death," I said to myself, "and still the certainty of dying cannot compare with the pleasure I am feeling. The joy I take from this half of an orange which I am holding in my hand is one of the greatest joys I have ever known."

The Feast

I lay flat on my back, sucking my orange and counting the shooting stars. Here I was, for one minute infinitely happy.

Wind, Sand and Stars
Antoine de Saint-Exupéry

From the sensual enjoyment of a piece of fruit to the sensual enjoyment of the universe, all in one short sentence. The leap is so natural we hardly notice it. We might gather that in the cosmic range of things an orange is not as small and insignificant as it might seem.

*J*oyful occasions are confirmed by food and beverage. A party just isn't a party without those ingredients. Tradition has much to do with it, but behind birthday cakes and shower mints and timely champagne is a natural propriety from which the customs evolved. When we eat and drink, we enact a mystery that is basic to our continuance on earth. We do it with little thought in that direction, but, discerning or not, we celebrate life by receiving into our mouths delicious tokens (more than we ought, sometimes) of that which we cannot exist without. Only to the believer would it make sense: Our joy is confirmed by a ritual signifying our dependency.

Some of our warmest memories center around feasts. They are warm because we hold them close, and we hold them close because the scenes are peopled with loved ones. Often the association between a dish and an individual is so direct that one is identified with the other. In my clan it's Joel's oyster dressing, Margaret's eggplant casserole, Alison's sweet potatoes, Laurie's vegetable quiche, Gene's fruit salad, Day's "Mother Hen." Among the blendings of friends and favorites are Victoria Hopper's rolls, Sally Pridgen's homemade sweet mustard, Susan Trautman's fudge. "We're having dinner at the Hastings' tonight. I hope that Ruth is making her Swedish meatballs." Not just Swedish meatballs, *her* Swedish meatballs. One especially good friend of ours died a few years ago, but she is represented at our table repeatedly when an elegant dinner is in order. Frances Meadows's poppy-seed cake, at our house, is never called anything but Frances Meadows's poppy-seed cake, because that is whose it is.

Some of our warmest literary memories center around feasts also. In stories as in real life, a bounty of food is conducive to geniality. It seems that we get to know the characters as family when we join them at a laden table. Somehow they become less fictitious, take on flesh and blood, when they eat and drink. In Charles Dickens's *A Christmas Carol,* the Christmas dinner at the Cratchits' is no less accessory to our perception of Tiny Tim's humanity than is his crutch. Can we think of him without catching an echo of that festive meal? Hardly. Or vice versa.

"There never was such a goose," Mr. Dickens tells us.

An overstatement, of course. And we are not to believe that never was there such a goose again.

For in James Joyce's *The Dead,* on a wintry night in Dublin in 1904, at the annual party given by Misses Kate and Julia Morkam, we come across a goose and entourage that is quite as memorable. Although John Huston's 1987 film (his last) did remarkable justice to the story, one could never go so far as to say that the camera bested the prose in capturing the aura of a feast.

A fat brown goose lay at one end of the table
and at the other end, on a bed of creased paper
strewn with sprigs of parsley, lay a great ham,
stripped of its outer skin and peppered over with
crust crumbs, a neat paper frill round its shin
and beside this was a round of spiced beef. Between these rival ends ran parallel lines of side-
dishes; two little minsters of jelly, red and
yellow; a shallow dish full of blocks of blanc-
mange and red jam, a large green leaf-shaped
dish with a stalk-shaped handle, on which lay
bunches of purple raisins and peeled almonds, a
companion dish on which lay a solid rectangle
of Smyrna figs, a dish of custard topped with
nutmeg, a small bowl full of chocolates and
sweets wrapped in gold and silver papers and a
glass vase in which stood some tall celery stalks.
In the centre of the table there stood, as sentries
to a fruit-stand which upheld a pyramid of
oranges and American apples, two squat old-
fashioned decanters of cut glass, one containing

port and the other dark sherry. On the closed square piano a pudding in a huge yellow dish lay in waiting and behind it were three squads of bottles drawn up according to the colours of their uniforms, the first two black, with brown and red labels, the third and smallest squad white, with transverse green sashes.

Gabriel took his seat boldly at the head of the table and, having looked to the edge of the carver, plunged his fork firmly into the goose. He felt quite at ease now for he was an expert carver and liked nothing better than to find himself at the head of a well-laden table.

"Miss Furlong, what shall I send you?" he asked. "A wing or a slice of the breast?"

"Just a small slice of the breast."

"Miss Higgins, what for you?"

"Oh, anything at all, Mr. Conroy."

While Gabriel and Miss Daly exchanged plates of goose and plates of ham and spiced beef Lily went from guest to guest with a dish of hot floury potatoes wrapped in a white napkin. This was Mary Jane's idea and she also suggested apple sauce for the goose but Aunt Kate had said that plain roast goose without any apple sauce had always been good enough for her and she hoped she might never eat worse. Mary Jane waited on her pupils and saw that they got the best slices and Aunt Kate and Aunt Julia opened and carried across from the piano bottles of stout and ale for the gentlemen and bottles of minerals for the ladies. There was a great deal of confusion and laughter and noise, the noise of orders and counter orders, of knives and forks, of corks and glass-stoppers. Gabriel began to carve second helpings as soon as he had finished the first round without serving himself. Every-one protested loudly so that he compromised by taking a long draught of stout for he had found the carving hot work. Mary Jane settled down quietly to her supper but Aunt Kate and Aunt Julia were still toddling round the table, walking on each other's heels, getting in each other's way and giving each other unheeded orders. Mr. Browne begged of them to sit down and eat their suppers and so did Gabriel but they said there was time enough, so that, at last, Freddy Malins stood up and, capturing Aunt Kate, plumped her down on her chair amid general laughter.

When everyone had been well served Gabriel said, smiling:

"Now, if anyone wants a little more of what vulgar people call stuffing let him or her speak."

A chorus of voices invited him to begin his own supper and Lily came forward with three potatoes which she had reserved for him.

"Very well," said Gabriel amiably, as he took another preparatory draught, "kindly forget my existence, ladies and gentlemen, for a few minutes."

The Dead
James Joyce

Can feasting be *Christian?* What about the poor who have little or nothing to eat? Should we not feel guilty when we sit down to a plenteous meal knowing that there are people in the world who are starving? The questions are fair and cannot be shrugged off complacently. On the one hand we see that God in the Old Testament ordained a cycle of feasts to mark the very cadence on which Israel's worship was based, and we note that John in his Gospel presents the earthly ministry of Christ in a chronological framework of those temple festivals, so we deduce that feasts and festivals are not improper, that indeed their first and most precise purpose is an invitation to rejoice in the Lord. On the other hand the fifty-eighth chapter of the book of the prophet Isaiah makes it clear that the righteous divide their food with the hungry and take the homeless into their houses. The eighteenth chapter of the book of the prophet Ezekiel declares the same requirement. And, according to Matthew's Gospel, the day will come when the Son of Man will pronounce, not as a gentle reprimand but as judgment, "I was hungry and you gave me nothing to eat."

We are called to the feast, we are called to the fast. We are called to rejoice in the Lord, we are called to empathize with the hungry. The truths and admonitions of Holy Scripture are time and again sharpened by counterpoint, and the believer must seek the tension, not shy from it, for only in a tug-of-war will the poise be found.

Brooke Foss Westcott, bishop of Durham in the 1890s, confessed that he never felt he was on safe ground theologically until he found the paradox. It would seem that we are on safe ground if our call to the feast reminds us of our responsibility to the hungry. But we must take a step further and acknowledge that some of God's children do starve, in blatant contradiction to the biblical premise expounded here. This throws us back upon the horns, back to that predicament where we must decide to love God or to hate God. To love God in regard to these exceptions is to surmise that, having been called to a fellowship of Christ's sufferings from which some of us have been spared, the hungry will eat and drink the more deeply at the Marriage Supper of the Lamb. For those of us who take the Revelation of John seriously, that climactic banquet has to be the feast-event toward which all other feasts tend.

Likewise it has to be the wedding-event toward which all other weddings tend. Which reminds us that Christ, early on, demonstrated his personal approval of wedding feasts when he showed up in Cana. His mere attendance was the least of it. The affirming action he took on that occasion is considered by some of his followers to have been downright reckless.

On the third day there was a wedding at Cana-in-Galilee. The mother of Jesus was there, and Jesus and his disciples were guests also. The wine gave out, so Jesus's mother said to him, "They have no wine left." He answered, "Your concern,

mother, is not mine. My hour has not yet come."
His mother said to the servants, "Do whatever he
tells you." There were six stone water-jars stand-
ing near, of the kind used for Jewish rites of pu-
rification; each held from twenty to thirty
gallons. Jesus said to the servants, "Fill the jars
with water," and they filled them to the brim.
"Now draw some off," he ordered, "and take it to
the steward of the feast"; and they did so. The
steward tasted the water now turned into wine,
not knowing its source; though the servants who
had drawn the water knew. He hailed the bride-
groom and said, "Everyone serves the best wine
first, and waits until the guests have drunk freely
before serving the poorer sort; but you have kept
the best wine till now."

This deed at Cana-in-Galilee is the first of the
signs by which Jesus revealed his glory and led
his disciples to believe in him.

John 2:1–11, NEB

In providing wine for a feast, Christ *revealed his glory*. It was not simply that he supplied what happened to be lacking. We do well to remember that our faith proclaims him as the one who arranged the situation to start with. If he and the Father are one, as he later announced, he assigned the particular insufficiency. He might have expanded the house to accommodate an overflow of guests or pulled money from thin air to help the host with the bills; but no, he knew what he was doing when he set the stage without enough wine, the beverage that would figure so pointedly in his discourses. The fact that this beverage gladdens the heart and yet expresses the sacrifice of the cross is absolutely essential to the drama.

Christ's concern for human hunger and thirst is an integral part of the evangel. Perhaps its most spectacular outcrop is the feeding of the five thousand, but it surfaces in a number of out-of-the-way places, sometimes so casually and quietly that we can miss it if we are not paying attention. One instance that makes the point as well as any other is when, immediately after raising the daughter of Jairus from the dead, he says, "Give her something to eat." Sensible, down-to-earth advice. Having been enlivened by the Word of God, she is subject to the mystery of her own existence. She is no different from the prophet Elijah: She needs strength for the journey ahead.

The last scene of John's Gospel is, significantly, a meal. It is lakeside, beautiful to picture. The sun is rising. The disciples have fished all night, and they are tired and their stomachs are empty. When they come ashore, they see a charcoal fire, with fish on it, and some bread. There, wreathed in the smell of food cooking out-of-doors at dawn, stands the crucified and risen Christ, the person whom John identified in his introduction as the Logos, the Word through whom all things were made. He says to them (and I believe he says to each of us at the beginning of every day):

"Come and have breakfast."

Part Two
BY WAY OF HUNGER

$\mathcal{M}$an does not live by bread alone."

Deuteronomy 8:3, NASB

This statement is so familiar and worn that today we scarcely feel its original impact. Not only has casual quoting diluted the thought, modern applications often tend toward facetiousness. One does not live by bread alone—one needs a little peanut butter and jelly on it. One needs this or that or the other, whatever the desire of the moment happens to be. While we might chuckle at some of the necessities proposed, we probably nod in agreement with the hope that "our daily bread" includes meat and potatoes and other components of a well-balanced diet. In either case, whether through banality or levity, we enforce our ignorance of the import of that which is other than bread.

The words were first taught to Israel early on. "And He humbled you and let you be hungry, and fed you with manna which you did not know, nor did your fathers know, that He might make you understand that man does not live by bread alone" (Deuteronomy 8:3, NASB). The text indicates physical bread—one does not live by *physical* bread alone—which in turn opens up the whole concept of a bread that is spiritual.

For the Israelites in the wilderness, the absence of food was the preeminent concern. The staff of life had been removed, and there was no way to remedy the perilous circumstances. Without divine intervention, they would die. People in such a predicament care not for the extras of peanut butter and jelly, for the frills, as it were, or for sex or power or wealth. They care not for public opinion or for condos in Florida. They care only for basic food and drink. They want nourishment, sustenance, survival. It is a proper obsession. They would trade all they possess for a loaf of bread and a cup of water, and it would be a reasonable exchange.

What lesson was God teaching? That we realize our radical dependence on God for our basic daily ration? A valid application, certainly, but not the most significant one. God fed his people with *a bread that they did not know.* Although this includes the fact of our dependence on Yahweh Yireh, the Lord our Provider, it travels much deeper. Physical bread is not the issue at all. It is merely the illustration. The lesson speaks of the essential core of life, indeed of the source of life. God fed his people with a mystery. Manna was the surface manifestation of substance beyond. On one level it functioned to sustain life at its most profane expression, a life that at best was limited. Its higher purpose was to point beyond the shadows of reality that we know to the unlimited, unshadowed reality that is.

Terms like *mystery* and *substance* and *reality* float around in our heads and mean nothing at all unless a definition can be approached by the bridge of an example. God used manna as a visual aid to instruct his people in a higher dimension of life, a dimension they couldn't see on their own. We read that manna tasted like wafers with honey. How gracious of God the Redeemer to reveal his truth so appetizingly, to drive his point home with a sweet flavor. The lesson of manna indicates that true delight is not in the taste of honey but in the Giver of honey. In other words, we are to understand that completion is not to be found in the creation but in the Creator.

Hunger is an eloquent reminder of our incompleteness. We should recognize, however, that to be incomplete is not necessarily to have fault. This is clear in the creation account. Adam and Eve were created with certain limitations. In fact, their attempt to overcome these limitations outside God's provision led ultimately to their demise. But despite the limitations of creation, God made a pronouncement of "very good." Creation was perfect within its own prescribed function.

That was the case with manna. It fell directly from the hand of a gracious provider. It matters not that the constitution of this heavenly bread can be discussed in very simple physical terms. One theory is that manna was the defecation of an insect. Even if so, the supply was no less miraculous. And it functioned perfectly within the intent of its supplier. It was not intended to be more than it was. It was designed to feed the physical body and to point to a higher reality. This it did.

It is important to note that manna was provided in the absence of anything else. The Israelites were accustomed to deriving their food from crops and animals raised in accordance with the normal functions of the physical cosmos. Their nourishment was the result of certain predictable interactions involving soil, seed, sun, and reproduction. They ate because they toiled, and God was "more or less" involved.

The Exodus from Egypt changed all that. The normal methods of obtaining food were no longer available. The mercy of God was clearly the only escape from starvation.

And the mere provision of bread was not the entire lesson. After all, the Israelites had witnessed more spectacular miracles than this. They had seen the plagues on the Egyptians as well as the parting of the Red Sea, events that had more Hollywood flair. Manna was a quiet miracle. As quiet as snow. It was completely God's doing, without any human agency. Its source was God and God alone. It was his bread, and as such it contained a communication of himself. The material was the translation of the spiritual. The texture was of food, but the message was of God. God had spoken (quietly this time) and it was evident: God himself is the giver of all that humanity needs, all that humanity is. Life could no longer be defined in terms of food and drink. It had to be defined in terms of its source.

*O*ur Lord Jesus Christ was thoroughly familiar with the truth that manna taught. In his deity he had written the lesson. In his humanity he became that lesson. At first by way of hunger.

We can hardly imagine being in the desert for forty days with nothing to eat while the devil calls together all the forces of hell in order to come up with that one temptation that would accomplish his purpose. Jesus hungered even as we would have hungered. His deity afforded his humanity no dulling of the pangs. But when he was asked to provide by supernatural means that which was not called for by the Father, he flatly refused. He knew that his physical need was not the important issue. The nourishment of the spirit must always supersede the provision of the flesh. Jesus was willing to give up that which was necessary for that which was more necessary.

It is apparent from Scripture that the children of God have never been quick to learn this valuable lesson. "Why do you spend your money for that which is not bread, and your wages for that which does not satisfy? Listen carefully to me, and eat what is good, and delight yourself in abundance" (Isaiah 55:2, NASB).

Since Adam and Eve, we have survived through toil. Labor is necessary in order to obtain food. What a waste to spend our sweat on filler and fluff. We kill ourselves to purchase that which cannot bring life. It looks like bread, but it's a fraud. It does not satisfy.

In our own culture we slave away hoping to purchase a little more than the next person. We pay for steak and eat Twinkies. We starve to death while growing fat on that which is not bread. Yet God proclaims that there is bread in abundance. It is good, it is satisfying. How tragic that we pour out our souls to gain more and more of that which has no substance. Manna is present, but we would rather starve.

The epitome of the starvation syndrome can be seen in the man known as the wisest who ever lived. Solomon withheld from himself no pleasure. He followed his every caprice. But in the end his words are astounding: "Thus I considered all my activities which my hands had done and the labor which I had exerted, and behold all was vanity and there was no profit under the sun" (Ecclesiastes 2:11, NASB).

He had come to see all as vapor. Where apparent substance had been, there remained only smoke. Hope had faded to despair. Here there was no bread, no manna. Here was the land of the feast of death. Here was the table of eternal hunger.

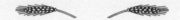

*T*he nineteenth-century French writer Barbey d'Au-revilly said that hell is the hollowed-out inverse of heaven. Employing the same kind of reference, we might say that hunger is the hollowed-out inverse of bread. In France, where bread is especially loved, there is the expression, "As long as a day without bread." I suspect that d'Aurevilly would have sanctioned my transference of his definition.

Why do we hunger? Certainly hunger itself is not the result of a sinful nature. Eating was a part of the world before the Fall. We are not to see our passion for food as some divine manipulation, with prankish gods watching us struggle through a wretched, meaningless drama. We are not to see existence as a routine in some sort of cat-and-mouse comedy. The human soul cries for more because it knows there is more.

Therefore we must not view hunger in negative terms. We delight in hunger when a feast is available. We even long for greater hunger when we behold an abundance of delicacies and have little appetite. And who would want to forgo the pleasant anticipation of dining with loved ones? Hunger actually works to our advantage.

Our understanding of hunger must go beyond the basic need for food. We long for more than earthly grain. What is it that produces in us a void that seems unfillable? It is a void of such enormity that our toil can only deaden the ache of the emptiness. Such emptiness compels us to consider hunger as metaphor. It points beyond its most obvious fulfillment.

If we hunger for a big meal and it is provided, we are satisfied. We think of food no more, until the cycle repeats itself. Implicit in this recurring hunger is an object that can satiate the desire. And what of passions that cannot be defined in such simple terms? The moment of pleasure slips away. After the moment of beauty, sadness. The return of the void. It is not always easy to spell out, but it is hauntingly present, calling for interpretation.

Just as we cannot precisely define this emptiness, we cannot fill it, cannot cure it. When we long for power, do we know how much power it will take to satisfy us? In our search for wealth, is there ever an amount that is enough? The winds of desire are always rising, often blowing with gale force, but what of the destination? Is there one? If so, is it known? That our prevailing hunger is a search for ultimate treasure there is no doubt. But how are we to understand this search?

Recorded in Genesis is an event that shook the foundations of human existence. In this event something was altered, something was lost that we miss in the very core of our being. We have never been the same since. It is in this event that we come to understand, somewhat, the hunger that drives us.

Now the serpent was more crafty than any beast of the field which the Lord God had made. And he said to the woman, "Indeed has God said, 'You shall not eat from any tree of the garden'?"

And the woman said to the serpent, "From the fruit of the trees of the garden we may eat; but from the fruit of the tree which is in the middle of the garden, God has said, 'You shall not eat from it or touch it, lest you die.' "

And the serpent said to the woman, "You surely shall not die!

"For God knows that in the day you eat from it your eyes will be opened, and you will be like God, knowing good and evil."

When the woman saw that the tree was good for food, and that it was a delight to the eyes, and that the tree was desirable to make one wise, she took from its fruit and ate and she gave also to her husband with her, and he ate.

Then the eyes of both of them were opened,

and they knew that they were naked, and they
sewed fig leaves together and made for themselves loin coverings.

Genesis 3:1–7, NASB

We tell this story to our children, in belief or dis-
belief, but even those of us who believe it have given
little consideration to its meaning. It seems that we
give consideration to everything except that which is
foundational. The average American knows more
about the crash of the stock market in 1929 than about
the Fall of man in the portals of history. Yet the hunger
of the Great Depression was but a minor representa-
tion of the one great loss that resulted from the event
in the Garden. Economic tumbles may come and go,
become old news, but that all-embracing tumble remains as current as our last disobedience.

In order to see the connection between hunger
and the Fall, we need to look at the event, the event
itself, and the history preceding and immediately following. It is best to begin with the creation of the first

man as recorded in the second chapter of Genesis. Here we find that Adam was not some casually tossed-off handiwork. He was not a snap-of-the-finger presence. Neither did he come about by fiat. God, who had created everything else by sheer command, was intimately involved in the making of man. The Artist carefully sculpted his masterpiece from the clay of the earth and then breathed the breath of life into him. The Eternal One personally and tenderly filled man with his own living essence. He himself was the life and sustenance of this new creation.

From the account we gather that Adam was content to serve his creator with no awareness of any poverty. He had glorious communication and fellowship with the one who had breathed the breath of life into him. He was without human companionship—a condition that would drive most of us mad in no time at all—and yet he seemed oblivious to the lack. It was God who recognized his need. He brought all the animals to Adam to show that man was unique and required a custom-made companion. He then in mercy provided the splendid creation we know as woman. The mercy is seen from God's perspective, for Adam had been content, was ignorant of his plight, had suffered no pain of want.

The beauty of the first man-woman relationship can be seen in the statement "And the man and his wife were both naked and were not ashamed" (Genesis 2:25, NASB). Total, unmitigated nakedness is a frightening concept. Exposure means vulnerability. Yet Adam and Eve in the beginning did not fear exposure before God or each other. Male and female enjoyed total nakedness—physical, mental, relational, emotional, spiritual—with no sense of shame. They could feast upon each other's nakedness in pure joy. Their condition was not one of naïveté but of innocence. Where there is no guilt, there is no shame.

The significance of God's personal involvement in the creation of Adam and Eve cannot be overstated. In chapter one of Genesis we learn that God created them "in his own image." There was a communication of divine likeness. To explain it precisely is beyond us.

The important thing is to catch a heightened view of our worth in light of our close association with the Deity. In some very important ways, we are a picture of God. We are the divine stamp.

Then came the event. Adam and Eve reached out in pursuit of personal deity. They chose to bypass God and set themselves up as divine arbiters. It was not sufficient that the image of God resided in them. In an act of cosmic treason they traded the command of the Sovereign One for the lie of the serpent. The distortion of truth promised they would "be like God." It was in this illegitimate pursuit that they traded their God-likeness for bondage. Human nature was never more unlike God than when our ancestors sank their teeth into the forbidden fruit. In their mouths was the taste of true death. Immorality had invaded the moral creature.

We don't have to look far to observe the results of that tragic event. We don't have to look beyond our own thoughts and words. But our focus here is on the immediate result. We are told, "Then the eyes of both of them were opened, and they knew that they were naked, and they sewed fig leaves together and made themselves loin coverings" (Genesis 3:7, NASB). The serpent was right. Their eyes were opened to a whole new realm. They now had a thorough working knowledge of sin. In their attempt to be like the God of life, they had brought on themselves and their progeny the opposite of life. In their mutinous eating of the fruit, they had fled from the God who had a right to rule. They had traded a freedom they didn't recognize for an imprisonment that we their children still cannot comprehend, or perhaps refuse to admit. What is the great predicament of humanity? Isolation. The first man and woman found themselves in circumstances they could not bear—they were that naked—and their only escape was to hide. We have been hiding ever since.

The father of our species found himself frustrated on all sides. His hiding was in vain, for he was hiding from the God who sees all. He blamed the Creator for giving woman to him. He blamed the woman for leading him astray. Expelled from the Garden and sentenced to toil, he found that the ground rebelled against him. He was alone in a way that he had not been alone in the beginning. We cannot imagine how cut off he must have felt. We are too used to the situation.

But we hunger for more than a regaining of the innocence lost when Adam and Eve feasted upon the tree in the middle of the Garden. As much as we desire to be free from guilt and bondage, this is not adequate to explain the insatiable longing that drives us in all of our ravenous pursuits. We are not simply hungry, we are famished. We have no idea how to satisfy the craving of our souls. Something happened in the rebellion that left us crazed with desire. We lost our bread, and we don't know how to get it back. In fact, we're not even sure what it looks like.

If we could rediscover this bread, we could discontinue our meaningless pursuits. We could settle down for the feast that is not a lie. We could know, at last, contentment.

$\mathcal{P}$erhaps the most telling clue to the identity of the sought-after bread was in the center of Israel's worship.

Then you shall take fine flour and bake twelve cakes with it; two tenths of an ephah shall be in each cake.

And you shall set them in two rows, six to a row, on the pure gold table before the Lord.

And you shall put pure frankincense on each row, that it may be a memorial portion for the bread, even an offering by fire to the Lord.

Every sabbath day he shall set it in order before the Lord continually; it is an everlasting
covenant for the sons of Israel.

And it shall be for Aaron and his sons, and
they shall eat it in a holy place, for it is most
holy to him from the Lord's offering by fire, his
portion forever.

Leviticus 24:5–9, NASB

The temple was the hub of Old Testament worship. There a whole nation of chosen people stood before the unapproachable Deity. This temple provided
the arena of reconciliation between the Most Holy God
and sinful flesh. Placed in the center of the activity,
on a table of pure gold, was bread: twelve loaves of
touchable, tasteable bread. There we see a meeting of
the spiritual with the physical, the holy with the profane. God met his people in bread.

It seems odd that amidst the gold and the fra-
grance and the sacrificial blood and the special garments

would be a substance as mundane as bread. How could something so everyday in character, so blatantly physical, signify something so profoundly spiritual?

Bread is more than the staff of life, it is the basic material of life. It is the solution to our most explicit hunger. With it we live, without it we die. Its presence in the temple signified, as did the manna in the wilderness, that God was the source and the power of Israel's nourishment on every level.

The representative character of that shewbread in the temple is indicated by the fact that only the priests, the representatives of the people before God, were to eat it. They alone were to approach God in things pertaining to salvation. When the blood of forgiveness flowed between God and his people, the high priest was there. When the bread of life was consumed in holiness, the priests feasted as God's people set apart. The direct connection between bread and salvation was celebrated instructively. It was not a meaningless display but an actualization of what was true.

In that rite Israel feasted on life in the presence of the God who *is* life. In other words, they feasted on God.

This kind of symbolism causes a tension to surface. Spiritual reality can never be fully contained within its metaphor, yet without the metaphor it can never be fully perceived. This necessary tension helps to develop a robust faith.

As a child growing up in Florida, near the ocean with its long flat horizon, I longed to be in the mountains. I liked the sun and the beach and skin diving and going out in the boat with my father to fish, but I liked mountains even more. Even before I had seen mountains for myself, I knew that I liked them. I felt that I could not live without them.

The day came when my family passed through North Carolina on the way to visit my grandparents in New Hampshire. I found the Smokies wonderful but strangely disappointing. They were not exactly the mountains I had longed for. I began to think of the Rockies. The Rockies were higher, weren't they? I looked forward to the day I could go to Colorado. Finally that day came, two weeks before I entered seminary. But despite my exhilaration as I beheld those loftier majesties, despite the joy I tasted as I hiked the ascending trails, I knew that the Rockies were not the mountains that would end my longing. I began to realize that even the Alps, even the Himalayas, would not satisfy me, that I was longing for a place I would not see in this life. That awareness was perhaps the nicest burden I carried with me to seminary. God was revealing himself in nature before he did in theology.

Inherent in the human breast is a dissatisfaction whispering that the grass is greener on the other side of the fence. Although it has prompted vain excursions since the beginning of the race, this dissatisfaction is in itself a clue to the reality toward which it reaches. The fact that we usually reach in the wrong direction does not mean that greener grass is a fiction. The intensity of the passion within us that keeps us searching affirms that it does indeed exist.

Higher mountains. Greener grass. In the long run, the search is the same. It's a cropping out of the hunger that is ultimate.

Why do we hunger?

We hunger because there is such a thing as bread.

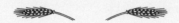

A hungry man eats and is satisfied. A widow in debt inherits a large sum of money and is elated to get out of debt. A soldier comes home from battle and cools his desires in the embrace of his wife. How long before the man will be hungry again? How long before the widow will be in debt again? How long before the soldier longs for his wife once more? The satisfactions were real and good, but they were not lasting. Food and money and sexual pleasure, mercies though they be, are not individually or collectively the feast for which the human soul hungers.

This tension between shadow and reality is prevalent in Old Testament prophecy. It had to do with one validity then and another validity later. When God spoke through a prophet, the people were to expect some immediate application—the "immediacy" of which might extend over decades or centuries—and yet the foretellings were still to find fulfillment in a messianic sense. The Israelites' release from bondage in Egypt prefigured the work of Messiah, who would come and deliver us from sin and death. Today, after Messiah has suffered, we continue to reel from the influence of those enemies. Freedom has come but not as it will come. The kingdom is here but not as it will be here. Fulfillment is both now and not yet. That is how it is with bread and hunger. We hunger for physical bread, and that hunger can be abated. But our deep craving is for the true manna wherein all longing is satisfied.

The New Testament bears this out with clarity. Jesus said to the woman at the well, "Everyone who drinks of this water will thirst again, but whoever drinks of the water that I shall give him shall never thirst, but the water that I shall give him shall become in him a well of water springing up to eternal life" (John 4:13–14, NASB). He used physical thirst and physical water to point to that which was beyond physicality. We are not to assume, however, that Jesus made reference to the physical in a depreciating way or that he saw it only as a springboard to the spiritual realm. He was not comparing the false with the true. He spoke of that which was real and that which was more real.

A metaphoric use of hungering and thirsting that brings us closer to this true bread and drink is found in the Beatitudes. "Blessed are those who hunger and thirst for righteousness, for they shall be satisfied" (Matthew 5:6, NASB). Here we learn that no satisfaction of the desire for righteousness comes while we are hungering for something else. Jesus spoke of a person wholeheartedly engaging in a particular pursuit and, as a result, finding what was longed for. Most pursuits that promise satisfaction do not deliver. But God assures this one.

The object of the authentic search is not happiness but completion. It is not personal peace (though that would follow) but a fulfillment of purpose. The goal is to arrive at the destination for which the human creature was ordained. Something is missing, and we hunger for it. Jesus said it can be found in the pursuit of righteousness.

This concept is not exclusively Christian. Most religions are concerned with purity—purity of mind, body, or spirit. The methodologies of cleansing include fasts and meditation and self-denials of many kinds. Purity is the motive, no matter how distorted it all becomes.

So Jesus in making such a statement was not saying anything that the human spirit does not in some sense already know. Yet he was saying something that opposes all human inclination. We hunger for that which will satisfy, but we feed for the most part on that which will not. We fill up on sawdust while snacking on steak. Our lives are spent in selfish pursuits, although occasionally we attempt an act of righteousness to satisfy our conscience. That minute satisfaction can be a deadly enemy, for it obscures the fact that we are starving to death.

According to Jesus, God has intended us mortals to feed on steak—or, in our context, bread. Again and again in the Gospels he implies the equation: bread is righteousness, righteousness is bread. This righteousness is not a mere abstraction that reveals itself in certain acts we define as right. Scripture defines it as something intimately involved with God's own character, with his own person. The quality Jesus spoke of cannot be separated from God as a self-subsisting entity. That is why those who pursue it without reference to the great I AM of the Bible will find themselves feasting on despair.

*T*he pursuit of the bread that is lasting is complicated by the legacy of our historical flight from holiness. In the Fall, humanity's character changed. Human beings did not become sinners by practice alone; they became sinners by nature.

"The heart is more deceitful than all else and is desperately sick; who can understand it?" (Jeremiah 17:9, NASB). "There is none righteous, not even one" (Romans 3:10, NASB). "[We] lived in the lusts of our flesh, indulging in the desires of the flesh and of the mind, and were by nature children of wrath" (Ephesians 2:3, NASB).

Enough! This dark progression of verses is sufficient to make the point: Human beings do not possess
and are incapable of generating adequate righteousness. God demands perfection, setting up his own divine nature as the standard, and we find ourselves in a
desperate situation. It all sounds terribly unfair. How
could God demand something that is impossible?

But to accuse God of unfairness, we must prove
that he has been inconsistent with his own nature as
the standard he demands. We must show that he has
violated the very righteousness that he requires of us.
This we cannot do.

Fault does not lie in the Creator. Nor does it lie
in the creation per se. "God saw all that he had made,
and behold, it was very good" (Genesis 1:31, NASB).
Adam and Eve in the beginning had the ability and the
propensity to be righteous. They could do exactly what
God demanded of them. The problem arose when they
turned from God and forfeited that ability. They could
no longer keep the standard. We have inherited their
loss, and we have no more right to cry "Unfair!" than

if we had inherited our immediate father's big nose or baldness or tendency toward cancer. Or, closer to the true situation, no more right than if he had squandered a fortune before our birth into poverty.

God, to be consistent with his character, must continue to demand conformity to the unchanging standard. Violation must result in judgment. If God fails to judge, he himself is the violator.

But the Creator and Judge is also the Redeemer. "His mercy is over all his works" (Psalm 145:9). Where we have come up short, God has supplied. He is not only the standard, he is the provider. Our want of righteousness is met in the incarnate, sinless, dying, resurrected, ascended, reigning Christ. The penalty for our violations was met in his dying. The pardon for our violations was ensured in his resurrection. The overall triumph was ratified in his ascension and continues to be ratified in his reign.

It might seem that this discussion of righteousness has taken us from our theme of bread. But no, it has taken us to the very center of it. Our need of righteousness is what makes our hunger pains so acute. We cannot hope to feast on mere sinlessness and be satisfied. Our hunger is not for some sterile code of goodness. The famished can never find wholeness in a rule or standard. Personality can never be brought to completion by the impersonal. If the human soul is to know fulfillment, it must be found *in a person*.

Can contentment be found, then, in human relationships? Many a love song would have us think so. But have you noticed that there seem to be fewer and fewer love songs? Songwriters have gone the way that many philosophers have gone. The way of hopelessness. Despite the amount of energy spent on the great search, the failure of human relationships to bring ultimate contentment is all around us.

We are finite by virtue of our humanity and imperfect by virtue of our fallenness. The cure for the finite imperfect person who is starving for true bread cannot be found in a finite imperfect person. If there is hope, it must involve a higher reality, a reality that is personal and infinite and perfect.

Man does not live by bread alone, but man lives by everything that proceeds from the mouth of the Lord" (Deuteronomy 8:3, NASB).

While acknowledging the necessity of physical bread this verse puts the need in its proper place by juxtaposing it with the revelation of God. Without the revelation of God, we are incomplete, empty, lacking. There is not only the body to feed, there is the spirit, which cannot be fed by the material. God proved to the Israelites during a forty-year school in the wilderness that he is the one who sustains the body. Implicit in that demonstration is the lesson that he is the source of all of life, and only he can sustain it in all of its manifestations. Our spiritual lives, as well as our physical lives, are just that: manifestations of his life. Within God alone is to be found the highest nourishment, the true substance, the true bread.

With this pronouncement God encouraged his people to obey the law. The Israelites were not to be governed by the laws of the flesh. To survive for the purpose of feeding the body alone is beneath the dignity of man. How could he who was created in the very image of the Holy One have no higher purpose than the gathering of a few temporal snacks? For humans to forfeit their position by feeding on their own law is a totally empty sacrifice.

The bare commandment of God, however, is not the true bread. It is necessary, but it is only instruction. The fact that the law of God proceeds from eternal deity establishes it as higher than other laws, but we are not to equate stark Thou shalt nots with the infinite, perfect personality that is essential for our total nourishment. We need to recognize that the law contains and expresses the character and attributes of that one, infinite, perfect personality.

While reading the Psalms one cannot help but notice the amount of space devoted to the law of God. I find it interesting that "O how I love thy law!" (Psalm 119:97, NASB) is the theme of the longest psalm. The psalmist did not seek to cast off the commands of God as a slave longs to cast off the fetters of his imprisonment. Quite the contrary, he pursued God's law as one pursues great treasure. "My soul is crushed with longing after Thine ordinances at all times" (Psalm 119:20, NASB). This is hunger of the highest order. This is passion for truth. The psalmist longs for the bread of life and seeks it in the mouth of God.

"How blessed are those who observe his testimonies, who seek him with all their heart" (Psalm 119:2, NASB). Here the psalmist identifies the observance of the law as the pursuit of God himself. The substance of life is not found in adherence to a standard. The goal is not perfect obedience to the law (although that is required) but the seeking of the person of God. "As the deer pants for the waterbrooks, so my soul thirsts for Thee, O God. My soul thirsts for God, for the living God" (Psalm 42:1–2, NASB). Whimsical language? No. Neither is it hyperbole. The writer is a poet using the strongest language available to him to express the longing of the soul. As the dry, dusty tongue craves to be refreshed with water, the dry, dusty soul longs to be immersed in God.

God made us: invented us as a man invents an engine. A car is made to run on gasoline, and it would not run properly on anything else. Now God designed the human machine to run on Himself. He Himself is the fuel our spirits were designed to burn, or the food our spirits were designed to feed on. There is no other.

Mere Christianity
C. S. Lewis

This is our hope: to feed on him. In him alone is life. He is the unlimited, unchanging personality that can satisfy the longings and needs of humankind. He is the essence of our being, the core of our existence. Ultimately, to feed on anything else is vain mastication. The stomach may be full, but the being is malnourished and in time will die.

For one to feast on God, one must do so in consistency with the divine nature. It is impossible to have dealings with a righteous, pure, holy God in an unrighteous, impure, and unholy way. Without communication in some form, two beings are incapable of relations. How foolish of us to believe that by scientific examination or unguided mystic inquiry the infinite can be found out. The Creator knows the created intimately, but the Creator is known by the created only to the extent that the Creator deigns to reveal himself. Without revelation there is no knowledge of God. To feast on God is therefore impossible without the Word of God.

The Word of God goes beyond the stone tablets of Sinai and the leafy pages of the Bible. These manifestations offer the scent of food, and lead us to it, but are not in themselves the nourishment of the soul. The infinite God surpasses human language. That ought to go without saying. The beginning of the Fourth Gospel is about as close as we can come to the mystery of revelation: "In the beginning was the Word, and the Word was with God, and the Word was God" (John 1:1, KJV).

In creation the Word was already operative, calling forth, ordering, forming, revealing. The Word is the paradigm of revelation—in nature and in grace. Unfortunately the created world took on imperfection as a result of the Fall. The Word Incarnate is the flawless exposure of the flawless God. The Word is a person "who, though he was in the form of God, did not regard equality with God as something to be exploited, but emptied himself, taking the form of a slave, being born in human likeness" (Philippians 2:6–7, NRSV). The Word of God is the bridge between the infinite and the finite, the portal through the impasse separating the holy from the profane.

God has spoken. God continues to speak. His Word is ever new. Because of this most important communication, we are no longer lonely.

But—think about it—we are still hungry, are we not?

We stand at a fork in the road.

In one direction we see a wide path—we might even call it a boulevard—with many inviting way stations and markets along the route. Displays of merchandise beckon the eye. To look is to want. But to have is to hunger, for the wares offer but a hollow crust of reality. The things are real, but they are not real enough. They are not what life is about. There is a confusion of signs and a riot of buying and selling and trading. There are pursuits and goals and successes and failures. The activity simulates a large board game with innumerable pieces moving backward and forward, out of one loop and into another, around and around. The currents are strong and the finish is uncertain. It doesn't really matter where it all is leading. So many players couldn't be wasting their time. And after all, it's only a game, isn't it?

In the other direction we see a different kind of path. Yes, a narrow path. It is traveled, but not heavily. The footprints are few enough to be readable. The way is overgrown, the terrain is difficult. Blind corners await. There is only one sign. It reads: True Bread. The footprints tell us that many started down this path and then turned around and took the other one. They probably wore their play clothes, expecting to obtain the true bread handily, expecting to be on that path but a short while anyway, and we can picture them turning back, tired and empty-handed. The smells of the carnival have pulled them. Those messages of frying fat and spinning sugar have drifted over from the other path and masked the finer scent. But if one stands there and opens one's nostrils—if one concentrates—one can distinguish the smell of fresh, warm, lovely bread.

We understand, however, that the path itself is no picnic. Some of the persevering footsteps are deep and tilted, as if here and there a soldier had dug a secure stance to help him ward off an enemy. Clearly the path to peace and feasting travels the way of warriors. It is a battleground, not a playground. And the promise of great reward—is it only a rumor? How can one be sure that the goal is worth the struggle? It all appears quite chancy, as chancy as the game, and the game requires so much less from its participants.

Many a pilgrim has passed up God's bakery to feed on sugarcoated vanity. We stand at a fork in the road where a crucial decision must be made. In a sense we stand here at the beginning of every day. Down which road will we travel? What will we eat along the way? More to the point: On what will we feed when we reach our destination?

After feeding the five thousand, Jesus fled to the mountain to escape the people who wanted to seize him and make him their king. A prophet who could satisfy corporate hunger on that scale with only five barley loaves and two fish was the leader for them!

Their reasoning does not seem too far off base. But Jesus would have us know that it is.

When the multitude therefore saw that Jesus was not there, nor His disciples, they themselves got into the small boats and came to Capernaum, seeking Jesus.

And when they found Him on the other side of the sea, they said to Him, "Rabbi, when did You get here?"

Jesus answered them and said, "Truly, truly I say to you, you seek Me, not because you saw signs, but because you ate of the loaves, and were filled.

"Do not work for the food which perishes, but for the food which endures to eternal life, which the Son of Man shall give to you, for on Him the Father, even God, has set his seal."

John 6:24–27, NASB

At first glance the zeal of the crowd could be an example of great faith. They piled into boats and crossed the Sea of Galilee to get close to Jesus. They had needs, they had questions, and so they sought out the man sent from God. This seems rather commendable, but Jesus gave no commendation. He gave only rebuke. He pierced to the innermost intents of their hearts and laid bare their deepest motives. Their main desire was to fill their stomachs. They stood in the presence of holiness, yet all they wanted was another meal. The Ancient of Days had come, the hope of the ages, and all they could see was a means to another loaf of bread, another piece of fish.

Jesus was not primarily concerned with their hunger on the occasion of that miracle. He was concerned that they celebrate the Passover. What a wonderful opportunity this was. As they recalled the blood of the lambs that warded off the angel of death in Egypt, their eyes could be fixed on the Lamb of God who takes away the sin of the world. The Lamb himself was providing the feast. It could have been a time of great rejoicing and worship, but the crowd, settling for full stomachs, missed it. In the blindness of their reasoning, they were willing to content themselves with temporary hope for decaying bodies. Their attitude was like that of the widow in Elijah's day: "I have . . . only a handful of flour in the bowl and a little oil in the jar;

and behold, I am gathering a few sticks that I may go in and prepare for me and my son, that we may eat it and die" (1 Kings 17:12, NASB).

To toil for that which has no permanent value is to live for death and be blinded toward life. It makes no sense to store up food that will perish. That is what Jesus was saying to those who chased him down. That is what he was saying to all of us.

The one who fed the five thousand and delivered the rebuke the following day was the one who was capable of supplying the bread that would stay fresh forever. He was not a prophet instructing them where to find it. He was himself the storehouse. He desired to give them the food of eternal life. They were not interested. They were indignant because Jesus had treated them so harshly.

They said therefore to Him, "What do You do for a sign, that we may see, and believe You? What work do you perform? Our fathers ate the

manna in the wilderness; as it is written, 'He
gave them bread out of heaven to eat.' "

John 6:30–31, NASB

So near and yet so far. Jesus had just provided a
sign, and here they were asking for one. The feeding
of the multitude was a miracle and the multitude knew
it; but more importantly it was a sign, and they should
have known that. Jewish tradition foretold a second redeemer who would repeat the miracle of manna as performed by the first redeemer. Their reference to manna
indicates that they saw similarities between the miracle
of the bread that they had witnessed and the provision
of manna in the wilderness. How could they not see
that the long-awaited messianic appearance was now a
reality?

In their estimation, the work of Jesus was infe-
rior to the work of Moses. Jesus had provided ordinary
bread, and for only one meal. Earthly bread could never
take the place of heavenly bread, they reasoned. If

Jesus was to capture their devotion, he would have to go on and produce manna. Otherwise they would take such bread as he offered and be on their way.

Their attitude must have stunned the Son of God even though he knew they lacked vision. Could they really believe that Moses had produced the manna? Could there be any doubt that God was the source?

> Jesus therefore said to them, "Truly, truly, I
> say to you, it is not Moses who has given you
> the bread out of heaven, but it is My Father who
> gives you the true bread out of heaven.
> "For the bread of God is that which comes
> down out of heaven and gives life to the world."
> John 6:32–33, NASB

Jesus pulled them out of the past for a confrontation with the reality of God in their midst. It is too convenient to hide behind events that are removed by centuries. We all tend to do it, but God would have us involved with truth in the present tense.

In comparing the nature of this bread with the nature of manna, Jesus calls this bread "true bread." Here again the contrast is not between the true and the false. Both the physical and spiritual aspects of manna were a part of reality. But the highest reality was yet to be seen. The ultimate purpose of manna was to signal the nourishment to come. Now the goal of that earlier manifestation was finally at hand, and the fulfillment would far exceed any expectations that Israel might have held. This bread of heaven would provide life for a dying world.

The hunger pains throughout history were about to be answered in a single, simple, straightforward sentence. Centuries of thematic development were approaching their culmination in the setting forth of that which can satisfy humanity's deepest longings. The heavenly realm must have burst in a crescendo of exultant praise as the Son of God announced: "I am the bread of life" (John 6:35, NASB).

Considering the ordinariness of bread, his claim might seem to be no big deal, except to indicate the extreme downward reach of the Incarnation, which is a very big deal indeed. But considering the crucial importance of bread in the scheme of human life, the words might even sound arrogant if they had not been spoken by someone who was to be, like bread, broken and distributed.

What we have here is not a stingy God dropping down occasional crumbs to sustain a meager form of life. We have the God of the covenant entering personally into the lives of an ungrateful people, becoming flesh and bone and blood in order to feed them.

With this thought, we enter into deepest mystery. Science tells us something of how a crust of bread can sustain life. But what is to be made of this hard saying of Jesus? We are not especially comforted by his explanation. We might wish that he would pull back from the statement and weaken the metaphor just a bit, to soothe our intellect. But he does not do that. He does not back down in the least. He reinforces what he has said.

"I am the living bread that came down out of heaven; if anyone eats of this bread, he shall live forever; and the bread also which I shall give for the life of the world is My flesh."

The Jews therefore began to argue with one another, saying, "How can this man give us His flesh to eat?"

Jesus therefore said to them, "Truly, truly, I say to you, unless you eat the flesh of the Son of Man and drink His blood, you have no life in yourselves."

John 6:51–53, NASB

Do these words shock us?

Yes. But if we dismiss them, we dismiss the one who spoke them, the one who, when he was freshly born, was laid in a feeding trough—in Bethlehem, which means "house of bread." With that kind of symbolism in the nativity, I wonder why the reality of the matter is such a shock? Still, it is better to be shocked by reality, and to partake of it, than never to experience it at all. If we are sufficiently shocked, we will see our pursuits in proper perspective and, accordingly, begin to taste the Bread of Breads that is our salvation.

Part Three
A TABLE PREPARED

$\mathcal{A}$nd as they were eating, Jesus took bread, and blessed it, and brake it, and gave it to the disciples and said, Take, eat: this is my body.

And he took the cup, and gave thanks, and gave it to them, saying, Drink ye all of it;

For this is my blood of the new testament, which is shed for many for the remission of sins.

Matthew 26:26–28 KJV

If that which followed was neither cannibalism nor make-believe, what are we to make of it?

It would be interesting to know the thoughts of those present at the table. Jesus had said a lot of bold and startling things during the three years the disciples had been with him, and this must have puzzled them even more deeply. Yet, they simply obeyed: they took and ate, they took and drank, they did not clamor for an explanation. Furthermore, despite any unresolved questions that might have troubled them, they made the ritual of bread and wine an integral part of their worship after Jesus had ascended to the Father.

The metaphors by which Jesus had previously depicted his relationship with his flock were indirect and elusive when compared with the physicality of bread to be eaten and wine to be drunk. The idea that he was the true vine and they were the branches could be reduced to an abstraction and thereby kept at a safe distance; it did not have to be dealt with in a rite that required their bodily indulgence. It was as though the Savior had to identify himself with food and drink before he could fully characterize his connection with those he was saving. Perhaps no one has captured the impact of it so simply and yet so precisely as Mother Teresa in an interview with *Time* magazine: "Jesus made himself the bread of life to give us life."

To contemplate this statement is to enter the mystery that we must enter when we come to the Table of the Lord. We might even say that we must enter into ignorance. We can bring to his Supper every burden but the burden of intellect. It is not that we leave our intellects behind—we bring less than ourselves if we do that—but we must bring them humbled, empty of pride.

While some hold that the substance of the bread and the wine change at the time of consecration *into* the body and blood of Christ, some believe that the "true body and blood" are, by right of the Word, "in, with, and under" the natural elements. There are those who claim that the elements are merely fulfilling their original calling in creation, and there are those who prefer to see the mystery *as* mystery and avoid reducing it to a phrase or a formula. Others, attempting to re-move the scandal of it all, view the rite as a memorial only and the bread and the wine as no more than symbols. We, the authors of this book, recognize that all the angles down through the history of the church reflect sincere but faltering attempts to understand and implement this hard teaching of Jesus.

Unfortunately disputes about the matter have divided Christians for ages. Many a person was burned at the stake for upholding one view or another. Many a person is still looked upon as a lesser member of the body of Christ (if a member at all) for embracing a lower view (or, for that matter, a higher view) than the school that is judging. What a different history of the church might have been written if one devout sixteenth-century Englishman had been able to catch the hearts of all believers when he wrote: "What these elements are in themselves it skilleth not, it is enough that to me which take them they are the body and the blood of Christ, his promise in witness thereof sufficeth, his word he knoweth which way to accomplish; why should any cogitation possess the mind of a faithful communicant but this, O my God, thou art true,

O my soul, thou art happy" (*Of the Lawes of Ecclesiasticall Politie,* Richard Hooker).

The underlying contention has not been beside the point, however. The Protestant stance has always been that the sacrament is not salvific in and of itself, but that the recipient's faith is necessary. The Roman Catholic position emphasizes that nature and grace are inseparable, that we do violence to the very principle of the Incarnation if we set out to isolate grace from the natural world in which God implanted it.

Another issue has been the use of the word *sacrifice* in regard to the Mass. It was used by the early church fathers to indicate an offering of praise, a symbolic offering of all they were and all they possessed, and indeed a commemorative offering of the body and blood of Christ. The Protestant mind, careful to maintain the once-for-all aspect of the paschal sacrifice as propounded in the letter to the Hebrews, rejects any notion of repeating what took place on the cross. A writer in this century explained his Roman Catholic slant in such a way that many Protestants are likely to agree, and in so doing, broaden their own view without compromising it: "And though his sacrifice was made in time, in the historical hour of his death, it is celebrated eternally, in the endless present. . . . In the eyes of God, the millennia pass away and vanish as a day, but the sacrifice of Golgotha remains. . . . In all eternity there remains but one true sacrifice, forever current in the words: 'Do this in remembrance of me' " (*The Lord,* Romano Guardini). These words ought to be comforting to any believer who understands that he or she cannot come into the presence of the holy God without an acceptable sacrifice, and that Jesus Christ is the totality of what there is to offer.

One result of the disputes has been the loss, for many, of the eucharistic aspect of the sacrament. *Eucharist* means "thanksgiving." It was the term by which the early church fathers spoke of the great mystery. Their witness is not to be taken lightly; their comparative proximity to the day of the cross suggests a certain authority; among them were the men who distilled from the New Testament the doctrines of the Trinity and the Incarnation. They understood the central rite of the church in a context of gratitude. The other terms that have come down to us—the Lord's Supper, Holy Communion, Mass, the Divine Liturgy, and so forth—do not on their own connote that historical perspective.

There is a pleasing integrity in the term *Eucharist,* and it is significant theologically. The term applies to the sacramental elements as well as to the structure of worship in which they are consecrated and distributed. This integrity, expanding beyond semantics, beyond ceremony, into a view of all of life, is vital to the Eastern Orthodox tradition, which treasures a direct line of descent from the earliest of the Fathers. Perceiving the fullness of the sacrifice of Christ to include the redemption of matter, as indicated in the first chapter of the letter to the Colossians, Orthodoxy sees the miracle of the Eucharist not so much as a change per se but as the actualization in bread and wine of that which is indeed true. A leading spokesman for Orthodoxy in recent years defined the Eucharist as

> an entrance into a fourth dimension which allows us to see the ultimate reality of life. It is not an escape from the world, rather it is the arrival at a vantage point from which we can see more deeply into the reality of the world. . . . But as we stand before God, remembering all that he has done for us, and offer to Him our thanksgiving, we inescapably discover that the content of all this thanksgiving is Christ. All remembrance is ultimately the remembrance of Christ, all thanksgiving is finally thanksgiving for Christ.
>
> *For the Life of the World*
> Alexander Schmemann

Is that stretching things too far? Not if the resurrection is true. Our imaginations have to be enlarged before our faith can lay hold of such an encompassing Eucharist.

This is the kind of thanksgiving offered by those who recognize that the holy gifts of bread and wine signify the restored universe as eloquently as they signify the body and blood of Christ. This is the kind of thanksgiving we all ought to offer. We can do so only by acknowledging that we are unworthy to receive that which has been given—which is everything, which is Christ.

In the Eucharist we enact our spiritual values, but we do so in a blatantly physical manner. Obedience to Christ is never abstract. In this case it requires that we do something downright animal: open our mouths. "When our Lord wished to establish a sacramental act through which men might know and worship him throughout the centuries, he fastened on food and drink as the medium. He addressed himself to man the eater, man the drinker—not man the thinker, man the artist, man the contemplative, but man the consumer of food and drink" (*The Offering of Man,* Harry Blamires). The Eucharist is the ground on which the distinctions between physical reality and spiritual reality disappear.

It is the balance point. Here we deal with the visible and the invisible without losing our equilibrium. Here is our sanity, if we but approach with awe.

To reclaim the sense of awe that has been bred out of us, we must put back together something that was torn asunder long ago. When Berengar of Tours in the eleventh century asserted that the presence of Christ in the elements is mystical and not real, the council that condemned him took the position of declaring exactly the reverse: The presence is real, not mystical. We bring this up not to argue on one side or the other but to point out how at one pivotal hour in history the realms of the mystical and the real were determined to be mutually exclusive. The impact of that hour in history has been as devastating to the world in general—and to Christendom in particular—as the splitting of the atom was to the cities of Hiroshima and Nagasaki centuries later. We are still crippled by the disconnection of what the early Fathers had seen as a unity. Our symbols have been divorced from that which they signaled. Had Saint Augustine lived to see the tragedy, he probably would have said that the sunlight might as well have been severed from the sun.

Is it possible to put this Humpty-Dumpty back together? Maybe not, so far as the culture surrounding us is concerned. But on a personal basis, yes, with the help of our God, who delights to perform miracles.

Where do we begin? With bread and wine. To be more precise, with thanksgiving and bread and wine. Thanksgiving precedes the miracle. It was so with the loaves and the fishes; Jesus did not pray for a miracle, he simply offered thanks and the unbelievable happened. It was so at the Last Supper. The order is perpetuated in the ever-prompting liturgy handed down to us.

The ancient beginning begins:

The Lord be with you.
    And with your spirit.
Lift up your hearts.
    We lift them up to the Lord.
Let us give thanks to the Lord our God.
    It is meet and right so to do.

119

$\mathcal{T}$hanksgiving is an essential, though often neglected, part of Christian life. The apostle Paul commands us to "give thanks in all circumstances, for this is God's will for you in Christ Jesus" (1 Thessalonians 5:18, NIV).

God's will for his people is joy. It is not that all circumstances bring joy but that thanksgiving does. Thanksgiving is our entrance into the joy of the Lord, "who for the joy set before him endured the cross" (Hebrews 12:2, NIV). Perhaps the connection between thanksgiving and joy is most obvious in the Psalms. There, time and again, the blues disappear with a celebrative recounting of God's mighty acts.

Thanksgiving was prescribed as a way of life for ancient Israel. It was ingrained in the culture. Contrary to a view of thanksgiving that involves but a casual tipping of the hat to God, Israel's thanksgiving incorporated a detailed and costly ritual.

It is in the book of Leviticus that we learn how God's people are to approach him in worship. Unfortunately this is a subject given scant attention in modern presentations of the gospel. Christ did not obliterate the principles involved if sinful humanity is to come into the presence of the Holy One. The atonement of the cross sharpened those principles. In Leviticus, where we learn about the meeting place between God and humanity, the doctrine of thanksgiving is not only introduced but is spelled out in exacting particulars.

On Mount Sinai, God instructed Moses in the sacrifices that the priests were to offer perpetually for the people. Leviticus 7:37 lists "the burnt offering, the grain offering, the guilt offering, the ordination offering, and the sacrifice of peace offerings" (NASB). The peace offerings were divided into a number of separate sacrifices and were designed for the specific purpose of rendering thanks for divine mercies.

They were similar to the other sacrifices in many ways, but there was a major difference. The calendar of God was very strict concerning the occasions on which the other sacrifices were to be performed. While the guilt offerings were flexible according to necessity, only the peace offerings were allowed a general freedom in obedience. Except for two required observances, they were not mandatory. They were prompted by a personal desire to say thank you to God. The grateful believer was provided a way to express joy and indebtedness. It was not possible for anyone to spontaneously atone for sins—or to atone for sins, period. Only the death of an innocent victim could do that. It was not possible for anyone to fulfill any of the other offerings by whim. But even within the rigidity of Mosaic law, the heart was allowed the spontaneous expression of worship called thanksgiving.

Our dwelling on this freedom should not blur the fact that thanksgiving was commanded by God. The choice had to do with *when,* not with *if.* The redemptive acts of God required a response, one that was physical as well as spiritual. There came a time, however, when God was displeased with the sacrifices of Israel because a proper attitude of the heart was missing. We must remember that heartless sacrifices are no less dangerous than sincerity unmanifested. "Faith, if it has no works, is dead, being by itself" (James 2:17, NASB). In that regard, we might say that gratitude without expression is nonsense.

The importance of thanksgiving as a basic principle in Israel's worship is seen not only in the sacrifices themselves but in the prescribed involvement of the Levites, the priests. "He appointed some of the Levites to minister before the ark of the Lord, to make petition, to give thanks, and to praise the Lord, the God of Israel" (1 Chronicles 16:4, NIV). The connection of the Levites implies that thanksgiving is among the holiest of activities, since it was precisely the holy things that were assigned to their care.

Sacrifices of thanksgiving did not cease with the days of Moses. David, the great king of Israel, took care to ensure that the people of God were given ample opportunity, and ample reminders, to follow in this tradition. One glorious occasion on which he demonstrated his own gratitude was the return of the ark of the covenant, after long exile, to the place where it belonged. Thanksgiving broke forth into motion as he danced before the ark. The presence of God was back in the midst of his people, and that was reason for flamboyant rejoicing. Besides the gratuitous burnt offerings and peace offering, David appointed the Levites to offer up thanksgiving and praise with a psalm accompanied by lutes and harps and cymbals and trumpets. For David it was not a time to quietly slump over in a pew and offer up cerebral appreciation. He danced before the ark because it was time for dance. He ordered a symphony because it was time for a symphony. All of his senses were called to the event.

Certainly the psalms that David composed are brimming with thanks. "The Lord is my strength and my shield; my heart trusts in him, and I am helped. My heart leaps for joy and I will give thanks to him in song" (Psalm 28:7, NIV). "I will give you thanks in the great assembly; among throngs of people I will praise you" (Psalm 35:18, NIV). "Enter his gates with thanksgiving and his courts with praise; give thanks to him and praise his name" (Psalm 100:4, NIV). These are but samplings from the mighty tide of gratitude that rises in much of David's poetry. Down through the ages, the church, in prayer and practice, has benefited from the legacy of thanksgiving bequeathed by the one whom God identified as a man after his own heart.

King Solomon, following his father's lead, assembled Israel for the dedication of the holy temple and the placing of the ark of the covenant in its rightful station in the Holy of Holies. On that occasion the priests and the musicians and the Levitical singers joined in unison to offer up a sacrifice of praise with the exultant Psalm 136, the Great Hallel. At the sound of their joy and thanksgiving, the glory of God filled the temple so brilliantly that they all were forced to retreat. And so was confirmed, visually, dramatically, the phrase of David, "Thou who inhabits the praises of Israel."

The dividing of the kingdom of Israel and the deportation of God's people into a foreign land did not erase the necessity of thanksgiving. When the Jerusalem wall was restored under the leadership of Nehemiah, large choirs were gathered for a celebration of gladness and a lifting of thanks. As with the previous instances, the demonstration of gratitude was not compelled by law but by a true understanding of who is the giver of all good things.

When we come to the New Testament, we find that the importance of offering thanks does not diminish. The trappings change a bit when the temple sacrifices have been fulfilled and are no more, but the theme actually enlarges. The teaching of the apostles, the substance of which is Christ, is characterized by continuous thanksgiving.

Our Lord knew what the redemptive work of God would cost him personally. Even in those events that reminded him acutely of the price he would pay, he expressed a spirit of gratitude. In every breaking of bread he must have glimpsed the breaking of his body, and yet he offered thanks.

As we noted earlier, his offering of thanks before breaking the bread of the Last Supper was strangely connected with the approaching hour when he would be lifted up and his life poured out as a gift. We can imagine all of Israel offering thanks had they understood the nature of the sacrifice at hand. What we cannot imagine—it is too holy for us—is the Sacrificial Lamb himself offering thanks. But he did. His focus no doubt went beyond the plane of the bread and the wine and the confused disciples, beyond the shadowed room and the impending agony, to the Father's will that waited in the hearts of all the generations who would receive forgiveness of sins. His thanksgiving, which is ultimately our thanksgiving, came at great cost. The expense of those who in previous centuries presented the best of their flocks did not begin to compare.

It is true that in the New Testament there is less emphasis on the link between thanksgiving and sacrifice, but we are not to conclude from this that the concept is weakened or that our "spiritual" sacrifices are to be offered cheaply. In the days of the actual practice, only those who met the requirements of expiation and consecration could offer up a sacrifice of thanksgiving. When the repetitive shedding of blood was no longer necessary, the principle remained. Our peace offerings now—our thanksgivings—are as closely associated with the cross as those under the old system were associated with its prefiguring altars. Acceptable thanksgiving still requires redemption. Forgiveness of sins is still very much to the point in any transaction with our God who is holy. How fortunate we are that the sacrifice of Christ is available, always there to rouse our thanksgiving, always there to validate it.

We observe that the terminology of the old system is not discarded. We are to "offer up spiritual sacrifices acceptable to God through Jesus Christ" (1 Peter 2:5, NASB), "present [our] bodies a living and holy sacrifice" (Romans 12:1, NASB), "continually offer up a sacrifice of praise" (Hebrews 13:15, NASB). The expression of true Christian life is to be consistent with an act of sacrifice, and thanksgiving is to be an integral part of the whole.

The apostle Paul indicates that not to offer thanks is a mark of rebellion and unbelief. In Ephesians 5:4 we find a telling contrast: Thanksgiving is to be practiced *instead of* "filthiness." In 2 Timothy 3:2 we see that failure to offer thanks is cataloged as one of the results of unrighteousness. Thus we are reminded that those born of the Spirit are to be exemplary in disciplines of gratitude.

Thanksgiving ought to come as naturally as breathing. It ought to work the same way, like a bellows. In and out. Inhale the love of God and exhale thanksgiving. The problem is that thanksgiving runs contrary to all that evil accomplished in the Fall. To come anywhere close to getting it right, even with the help of grace, requires both passion and practice.

Exactly how are we to implement a comprehensive theology of thanksgiving down here where we live? Sufficient response to our Creator and Redeemer for the totality of his goodness would seem impossible. We are grateful not only for our food but for our families and friends and our houses and the pleasures therein and our cars and our jobs. Are we to send up some kind of thank-you note at every sight of a loved one? Are we to make an altar of our doorstep prior to every entrance? Are we to sing a hymn of praise as a prelude to the marital embrace? What about kneeling down beside the car every morning before climbing in and driving to work? Or raising our hands toward the sky before shaking hands over a successful business deal? Any of these acts would be fitting enough, but add them up and the sum of the ritual seems incongruous and out of balance with the existence to which we have been called.

Christians throughout history have used a pre-feasting prayer to symbolize thanksgiving for all benefits. Perhaps there is laziness in the custom, but there is also logic. Our daily bread is directly related to our being. Nothing speaks life quite like it. Family and friends and houses and cars do not sustain us as bread sustains us. We think that they do, but they do not. Bread is our hope for continuance. It is the nourishment of who we are. And as bread represents all food that is good for us, so a table prayer, sincerely offered, can represent thanksgiving for the whole gamut of essentials and extras. The Lord's Prayer is a miracle of compression, and so can our thanksgiving be. Another side of this is to realize that when we pray for our daily bread—when we pray for it intelligently—we are praying for all that is necessary for us to exist and operate.

Whether a table prayer is a thank you *for* the food or a request for God's blessing *upon* the food makes little difference. The first approach is implicit in the second. We are not proposing any one model as preferable over another. The child's "God is great, God is good, and we thank you for this food" goes profoundly in the right direction as long as the heart goes with it. Making the sign of the cross over a bowl of soup can turn a diner into a house of thanksgiving, because, properly understood, the cross is what thanksgiving is all about. We know an Episcopal priest who can change the entire character of a Big Mac by delineating a succinct cross in the air above it. (We asked him if he considers that too priestly an action for the non-cleric, and he replied with almost a laugh, "Why, the only right I have to the cross is that I'm a sinner.")

To endorse brevity, however, is not to depreciate full articulation. The long, capacious, detailed thanksgiving, whether prepared or *ex tempore,* whether majestic and cadenced or awkward and halting, is called for from time to time, in the same respect that a monument is called for at points along the way of any pilgrimage. All of us would do well on occasion to enumerate, in personal vocabulary, the blessings of God.

Perhaps the most beautiful expression of gratitude ever produced is the eucharistic prayer of John Knox. It is a loss in Christendom that most who follow in Knox's train no longer use his table prayer at the table of tables. We can only assume that at one turn or another it was deemed too long or too formal or, heaven help us, too grandiose.

It is for those very qualities, as balance, that we include here its final sweep:

O Lord, the blind dullness of our corrupt nature will not suffer us sufficiently to weigh these thy most ample benefits: yet nevertheless at the commandment of Jesus Christ our Lord, we present ourselves to this his table (which he hath left to be used in remembrance of his death until his coming again) to declare and witness before the world, that by him alone we have received liberty, and life: that by him alone, thou dost acknowledge us as thy children and heirs: that by him alone, we have entrance to thy throne of grace: that by him alone, we are possessed in our spiritual kingdom, to eat and drink at his table: with whom we have our conversation presently in heaven, and by whom our bodies shall be raised up again from the dust,

and shall be placed with him in that endless joy,
which thou (O Father of mercy) hast prepared
for thine elect, before the foundation of the
world was laid. And these most inestimable benefits, we acknowledge and confess to have received of thy free mercy and grace, by thy only
beloved son Jesus Christ, for the which therefore
we thy congregation moved by thy Holy Spirit
render thee all thanks, praise, and glory for ever
and ever.

Form of Prayers
John Knox

*D*o you remember the sumptuous meal that Babette prepared for Martina and Philippa and their guests? If so, you have read one of the finest short stories ever written or you have seen its honored film version, which is no less a work of art. What a wealth of insight is conveyed in that simple tale. Two unmarried Scandinavian sisters, raised to deny all earthly pleasure, give shelter to a French refugee and are recipients of startling grace when she spreads a bounty before them and their Pietist circle, forcing them to reconcile their severe Christianity with the goodness of the table.

Of what happened later in the evening nothing definite can here be stated. None of the guests later on had any clear remembrance of it. They only knew that the rooms had been filled with a heavenly light, as if a number of small halos had blended into one glorious radiance. Taciturn old people received the gift of tongues; ears that for years had been almost deaf were opened to it. Time itself had merged into eternity. Long after midnight the windows of the house shone like gold, and golden song flowed out into the winter air.

The two old women who had once slandered each other now in their hearts went back a long way, past the evil period in which they had been stuck, to those days of their early girlhood when together they had been preparing for confirmation and hand in hand had filled the roads around Berlevaag with singing. A Brother in the congregation gave another a knock in the ribs,

like a rough caress between boys, and cried out:
"You cheated me on that timber, you old scoun-
drel!" The Brother thus addressed almost col-
lapsed in a heavenly burst of laughter, but tears
ran from his eyes. "Yes, I did so, beloved
Brother," he answered. "I did so." Skipper Hal-
versen and Madam Oppegaarden suddenly
found themselves close together in a corner and
gave one another that long, long kiss, for which
the secret uncertain love affair of their youth
had never left them time.

The old Dean's flock were humble people.
When later in life they thought of this it never
occurred to any of them that they might have
been exalted by their own merit. They realized
that the infinite grace of which General Lowen
had spoken had been allotted to them, and they
did not even wonder at the fact, for it had been
but the fulfillment of an ever-present hope. The
vain illusions of this earth had dissolved before

their eyes like smoke, and they had seen the
universe as it really is.

Babette's Feast
Isak Dinesen

*It never occurred to any of them that they might have
been exalted by their own merit.* How's that for lively
Christian doctrine?

As soon as the video of *Babette's Feast* was re-
leased, a house we know (one of us happens to live
there) became a theater, open to all who would come.
The inherent theology in the story maintained its
force, showing after showing. One friend, watching
the film for the first time, spoke up and said, "Why,
that meal is having the same effect on them that the
Lord's Supper should have on the church."

Well said.

Babette's Feast, with its wondrous epiphany, surely
signals that greater feast to which we have been called
through the gospel. But so does the regular fare we
wolf down day after day.

The meal Jesus ate with the two men in the village of Emmaus on the evening after the resurrection was not the Eucharist, yet there is a direct connection: the liturgical formula of Jesus taking, blessing, breaking, and giving bread. He had walked with them along the road from Jerusalem and explained the Scriptures to them, and they had clung to every word and pressed him to come in for supper. But it was not until the moment of the breaking of the bread that they recognized him. They had been looking at him but not seeing him. As soon as they saw him—as soon as they knew him—he vanished from their sight. Those men wasted no time in leaving the scene of that "ordinary" meal. According to the historian's research, "They set out and returned to Jerusalem . . . [where] they gave their account of the events of their journey and told how he had been recognized by them at the breaking of the bread" (Luke 24:33, 35, NEB).

The principle of redemption is present in every bite of food that we receive with thanksgiving. One life was laid down for another. An animal was slaughtered.

A tender plant was ripped from the earth. Even vegetarians can't get away from the principle. "Whether the ox in the stockyards knew it or not as he was being hit on the head, or the kernel of corn as it was being pulverized at the mill, this is death in order that someone else (me) might live. It may be involuntary for this ox or this kernel, but the thing is at work nevertheless. . . . Life from death. The most sacred mysteries, shrouded behind smoke and veils and portals, and laid out there in your cereal bowl" (*Hallowed Be This House,* Thomas Howard).

Oswald Chambers, evangelical mystic, said that the Lord's Supper "is a symbol of what we should be doing all the time. It is not a memorial of one who has gone, but of one who is always here." What we should be doing all the time is doing all to the glory of God, Paul tells us in 2 Corinthians 10:31, and it's interesting that he zeroes in on the specific animal acts of eating and drinking as examples of that imperative. It is not by chance, but by his theology, that he uses them as a springboard to all acts of life.

In some liturgies there comes a point when the priest says, "The Mass has ended." With all due respect to prescribed forms and containments, the language is poor. When the Mass has ended, the Mass has *not* ended. Not really. Not for the believer.

Just as Sunday dinner is not really over when we push our chairs back from the table. The *work* of our nourishment has only begun. The result of digesting food is growth and energy and movement. The bread of earth, partaken in health, is to be fleshed out in physical life, and so is the Bread of the Gospel. John Calvin said in his *Institutes:* "Our Heavenly Father invites us to Christ, that refreshed by partaking of him, we may repeatedly gather strength." Strength is what is needed for activity, for industry. The Word of God, whether received through a verse of Scripture or through the Broken Body, is not to be reduced to nonlife. If it becomes an abstraction in our lives, we must assume it was received in ill health.

It's not just for *any* activity that we are fed the bread that is Christ. Immediately following the

141

monumental verse in which we are told that salvation is of grace and not of ourselves, we read: "For we are God's handiwork, created in Christ Jesus to devote ourselves to the good deeds for which God has designed us" (Ephesians 2:10, NEB). We are not to be an end in ourselves. We are to be useful—which, when we come down to it, means that we are to be used. Used by the one who has fed us of himself, to perform his deeds.

Good works is a catchall, and rightfully so, but as a term it usually doesn't catch enough. Although we should never soft-pedal its definition as acts of charity, we would do well to embrace in the category such things as good construction, fair deals, true measures, and the extra mile we are sometimes called to go without knowing why.

That acts of charity are considered high on the list is certainly in keeping with the character of the one who has ordained good works. A major proposition of this book is that a sound theology of physical bread will result in the feeding of the hungry. We would magnify the total Christ delivering the total gospel to the total person. A Christianity overbalanced on the spiritual side can topple into the kind of mission that might offer bread to the hungry only if they are receptive to a tract along with it. Every bit as sad, of course, is the mission that is concerned only with physical needs and disregards spiritual poverty.

It is easy to pray the Lord's Prayer and miss the connection between "Give us this day our daily bread" and the very next petition, "Forgive us . . ." We can be sure that they are linked by more than accidental phrasing. The two great needs stand together. Give us this day our physical bread, the thing our bodies cannot live without. Give us this day the bread of forgiveness, the thing our souls cannot live without. "All have sinned and come short of the glory of God," we read in Romans 3:23. Whether we call our shortcomings debts or trespasses, the vocabulary refers to the guilt which, if not dealt with at the cross, will blind us to the banquet now and exclude us from its ultimate fulfillment.

Hell, we suspect, is knowing that fresh bread is on a table somewhere and we must hunger for it eternally.
Heaven, on the other hand . . .

Acknowledgment is made for permission to reprint material from the following sources: Excerpts from *Waiting for God* by Simone Weil, copyright © 1951 by G. P. Putnam's Sons, reprinted by permission of G. P. Putnam Company; *One Day in the Life of Ivan Denisovich* by Alexandr Solzhenitsyn. English translation copyright © 1963 by E. P. Dutton & Company, New York, and Victor Gollancz Ltd., London. Reprinted by permission of Penguin Books USA Inc.; *Cathedral* by Raymond Carver, copyright © 1981, 1982, 1983 by Raymond Carver. Reprinted by permission of Alfred A. Knopf Inc. Copyright © by Tess Gallagher. Reprinted by permission of Tess Gallagher; *A Grief Observed* by C. S. Lewis, copyright © 1961 by N. W. Clerk, reprinted by permission of HarperCollins Publishers; *The Journals of John Cheever* by John Cheever, copyright © 1990, 1991 by Mary Cheever, Susan Cheever, Benjamin Cheever, and Federico Cheever, reprinted by permission of Alfred A. Knopf Inc.; *Bright Lights, Big City* by Jay McInerney, copyright © 1984 by Jay McInerney. Reprinted by permission of Vintage Books, a Division of Random House Inc.; *Wind, Sand and Stars* by Antoine de Saint-Exupéry, copyright © 1940, reprinted by permission of Harcourt Brace Jovanovich, Inc.; "The Dead", from *Dubliners* by James Joyce, copyright © 1916 by B. W. Heubsch. Definitive text copyright © 1967 by the Estate of James Joyce. Used by permission of Viking Penguin, a